T0084168

GRAPHIC HISTORY

THE BRAVE ESCAPE OF ELLEN AND WILLIAM CRAFT

by Donald B. Lemke

illustrated by Phil Miller, Tod Smith,
and Charles Barnett III

Consultant:
Lois Brown, PhD
Mount Holyoke College
South Hadley, Massachusetts

Capstone
press®

Mankato, Minnesota

Graphic Library is published by Capstone Press,
1710 Roe Crest Drive, North Mankato, Minnesota 56003.
www.mycapstone.com

Library of Congress Cataloging-in-Publication Data
Lemke, Donald B.
The brave escape of Ellen and William Craft/by Donald B. Lemke; illustrated by Phil Miller, Tod Smith, and Charles Barnett III.
p. cm.—(Graphic library. Graphic history)
Includes bibliographical references and index.
ISBN: 978-0-7368-4973-9 (hardcover)
ISBN: 978-0-7368-6203-5 (softcover pbk.)
1. Fugitive slaves—United States—Biography—Juvenile literature. 2. Fugitive slaves—England—Biography—Juvenile literature. 3. Craft, Ellen—Juvenile literature. 4. Craft, William—Juvenile literature. 5. African Americans—Biography—Juvenile literature. 6. Slavery—United States—History—19th century—Juvenile literature. I. Barnett, Charles, III ill. II. Miller, Phil ill. III. Smith, Tod ill. IV. Title. V. Series.
E450.L46 2006
306.3'62'092273—dc22 2005008084

Summary: In graphic novel format, tells the story of Ellen and William Craft's escape from slavery in Georgia to freedom in Pennsylvania.

Art and Editorial Direction
Jason Knudson and Blake A. Hoena

Designers
Bob Lentz and Linda Clavel

Colorist
Marty Van Dyke

Editors
Gillia Olson and Martha E. H. Rustad

Editor's note: Direct quotations from primary sources are indicated by a yellow background.

Direct quotations appear on the following pages:
Pages 7, 11, 13, 19, 20, 21, 22, 23, 24, 25, 27, *Running a Thousand Miles for Freedom* by William Craft (Athens, Ga.: University of Georgia Press, 1999).

Printed in the United States 5889

TABLE OF CONTENTS

CHAPTER 1

A SLAVE COUPLE

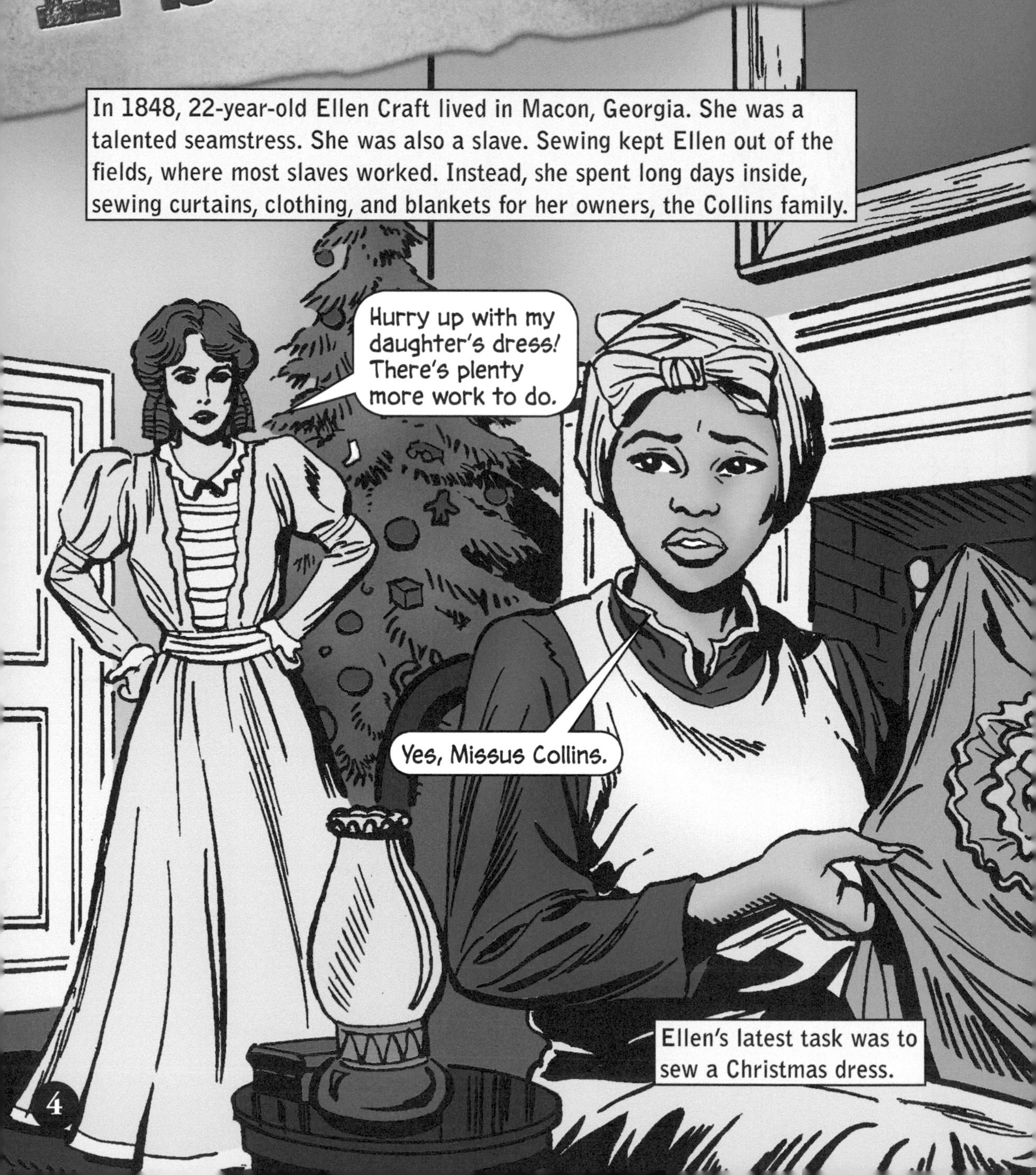

In 1848, 22-year-old Ellen Craft lived in Macon, Georgia. She was a talented seamstress. She was also a slave. Sewing kept Ellen out of the fields, where most slaves worked. Instead, she spent long days inside, sewing curtains, clothing, and blankets for her owners, the Collins family.
Hurry up with my daughter's dress! There's plenty more work to do.
Yes, Missus Collins.
Ellen's latest task was to sew a Christmas dress.

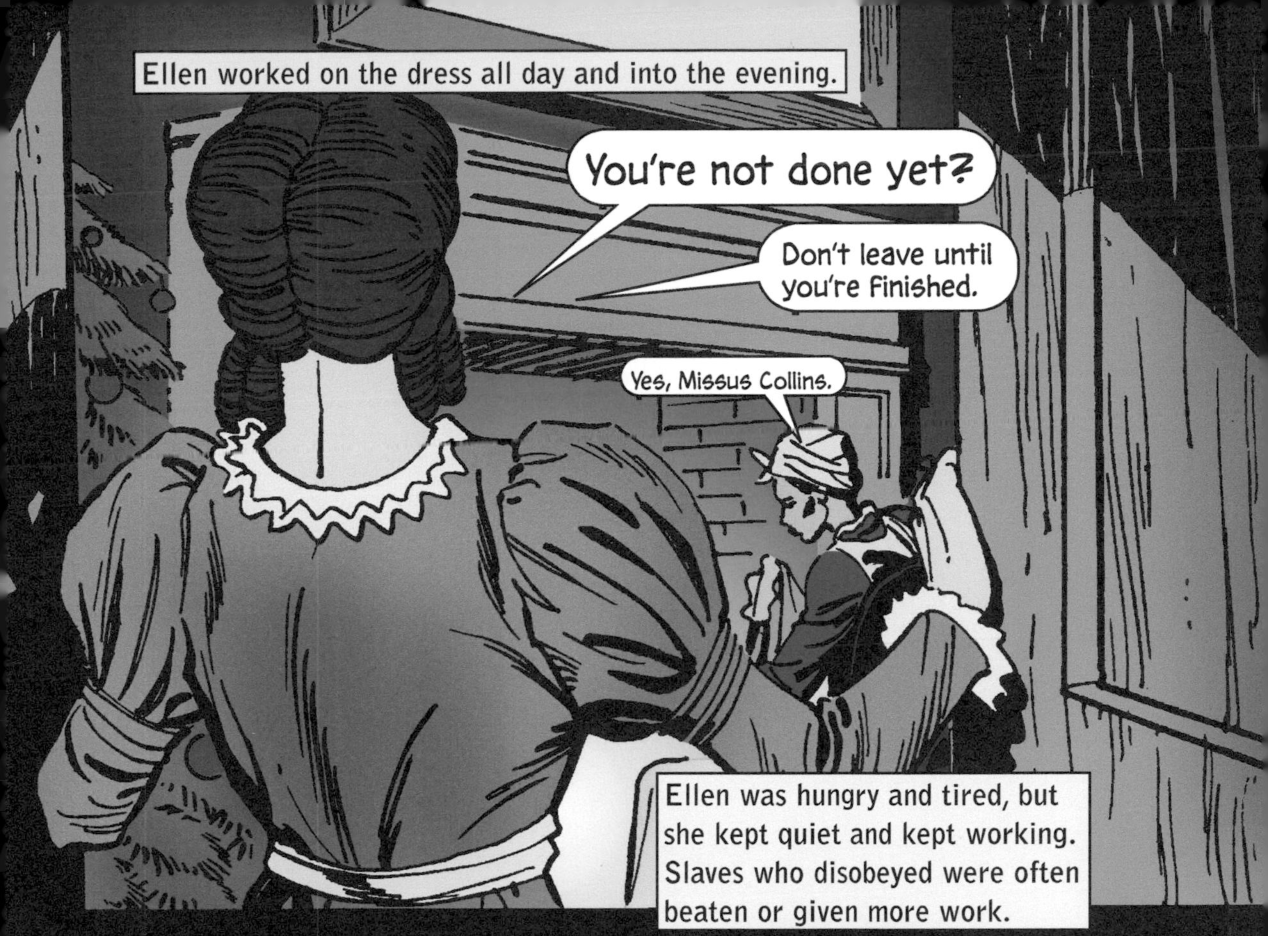
Ellen worked on the dress all day and into the evening.
You're not done yet?
Don't leave until you're finished.
Yes, Missus Collins.
Ellen was hungry and tired, but she kept quiet and kept working. Slaves who disobeyed were often beaten or given more work.

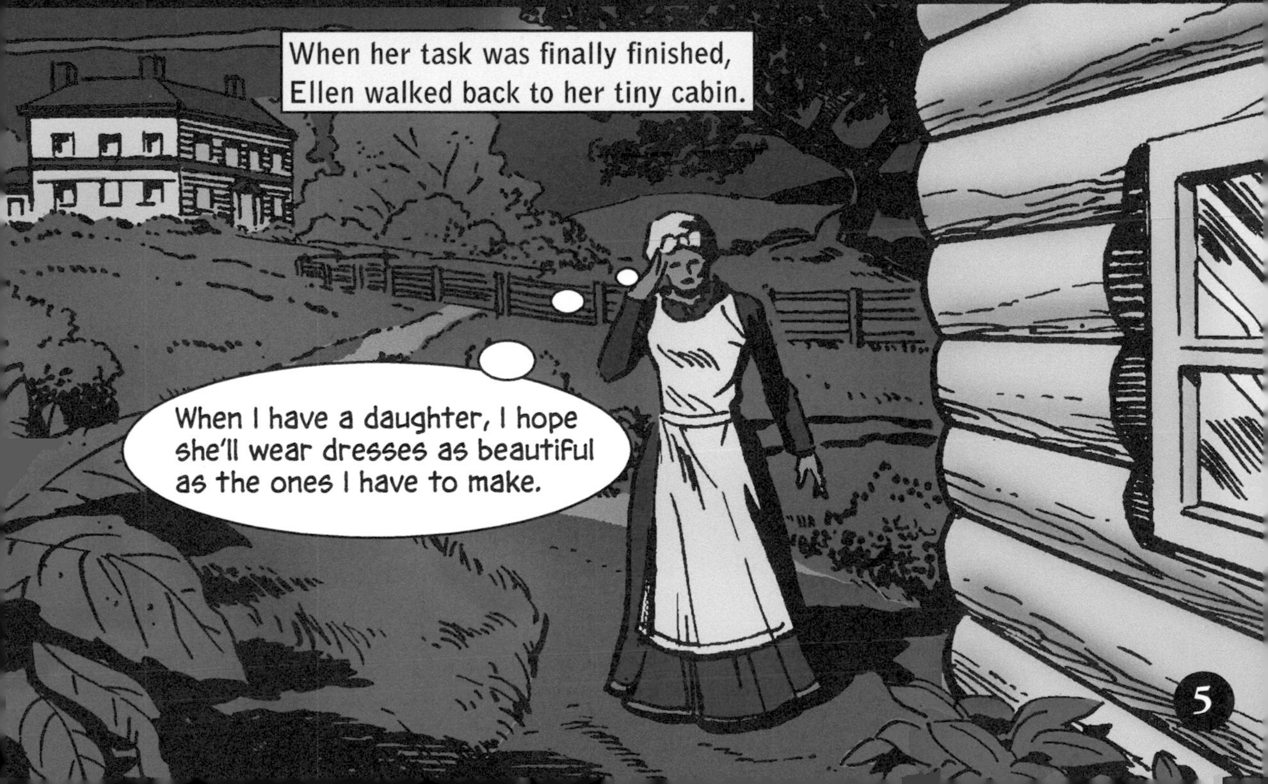
When her task was finally finished, Ellen walked back to her tiny cabin.
When I have a daughter, I hope she'll wear dresses as beautiful as the ones I have to make.

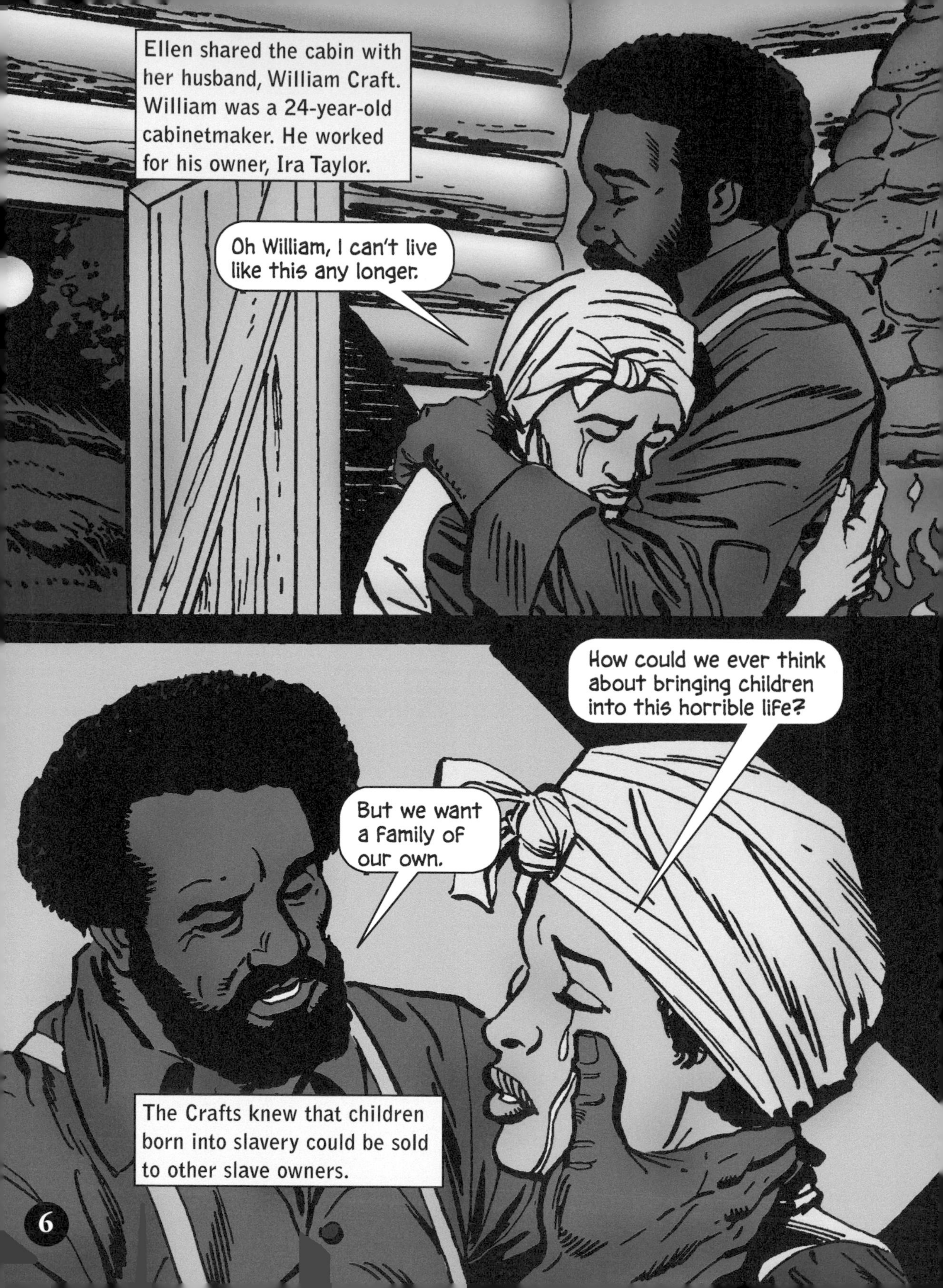
Ellen shared the cabin with her husband, William Craft. William was a 24-year-old cabinetmaker. He worked for his owner, Ira Taylor.
Oh William, I can't live like this any longer.
How could we ever think about bringing children into this horrible life?
But we want a family of our own.
The Crafts knew that children born into slavery could be sold to other slave owners.

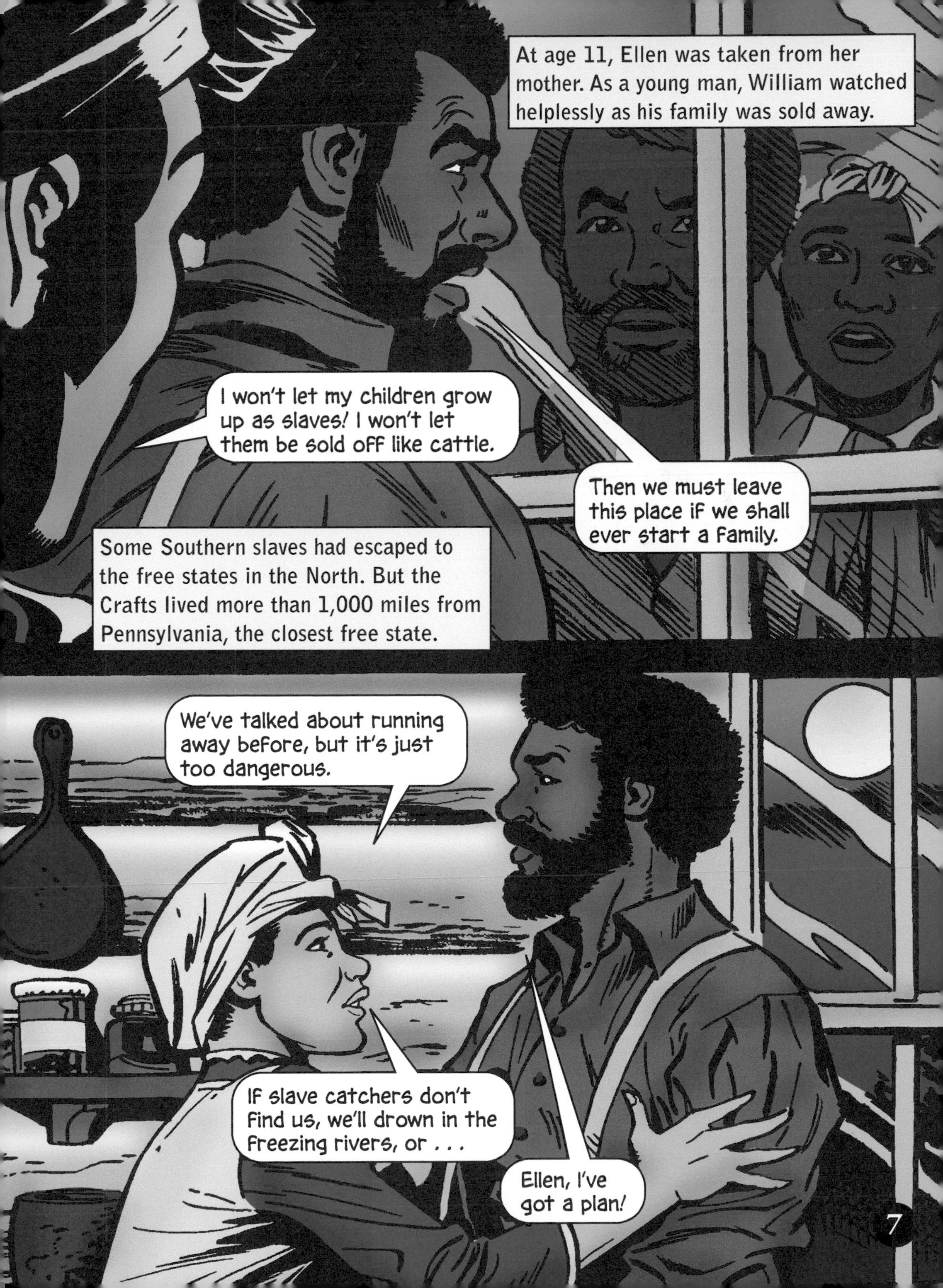

At age 11, Ellen was taken from her mother. As a young man, William watched helplessly as his family was sold away.
I won't let my children grow up as slaves! I won't let them be sold off like cattle.
Then we must leave this place if we shall ever start a family.
Some Southern slaves had escaped to the free states in the North. But the Crafts lived more than 1,000 miles from Pennsylvania, the closest free state.
We've talked about running away before, but it's just too dangerous.
If slave catchers don't find us, we'll drown in the freezing rivers, or . . .
Ellen, I've got a plan!

Chapter 2
An Escape Plan

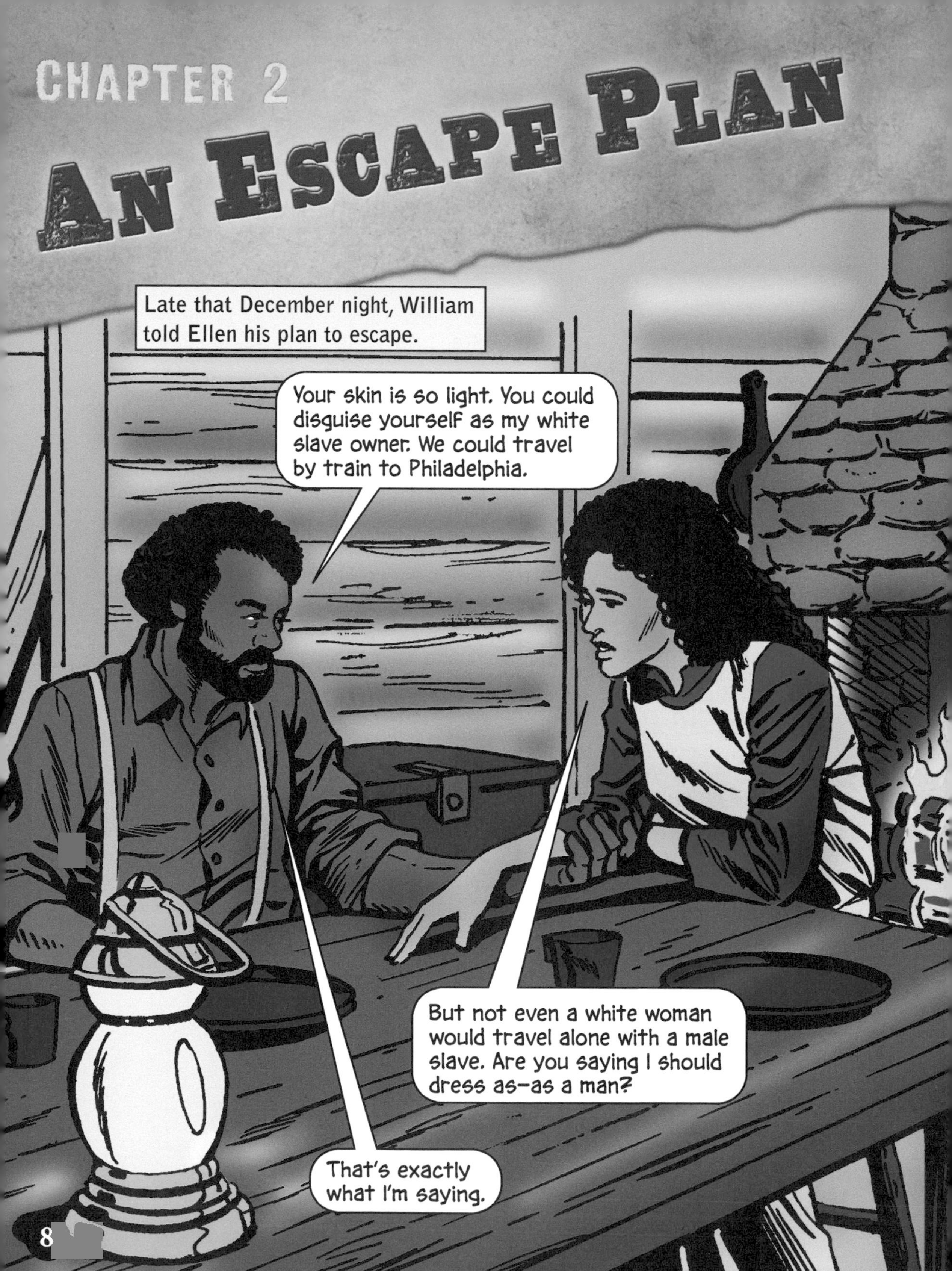
Late that December night, William told Ellen his plan to escape.
Your skin is so light. You could disguise yourself as my white slave owner. We could travel by train to Philadelphia.
But not even a white woman would travel alone with a male slave. Are you saying I should dress as—as a man?
That's exactly what I'm saying.

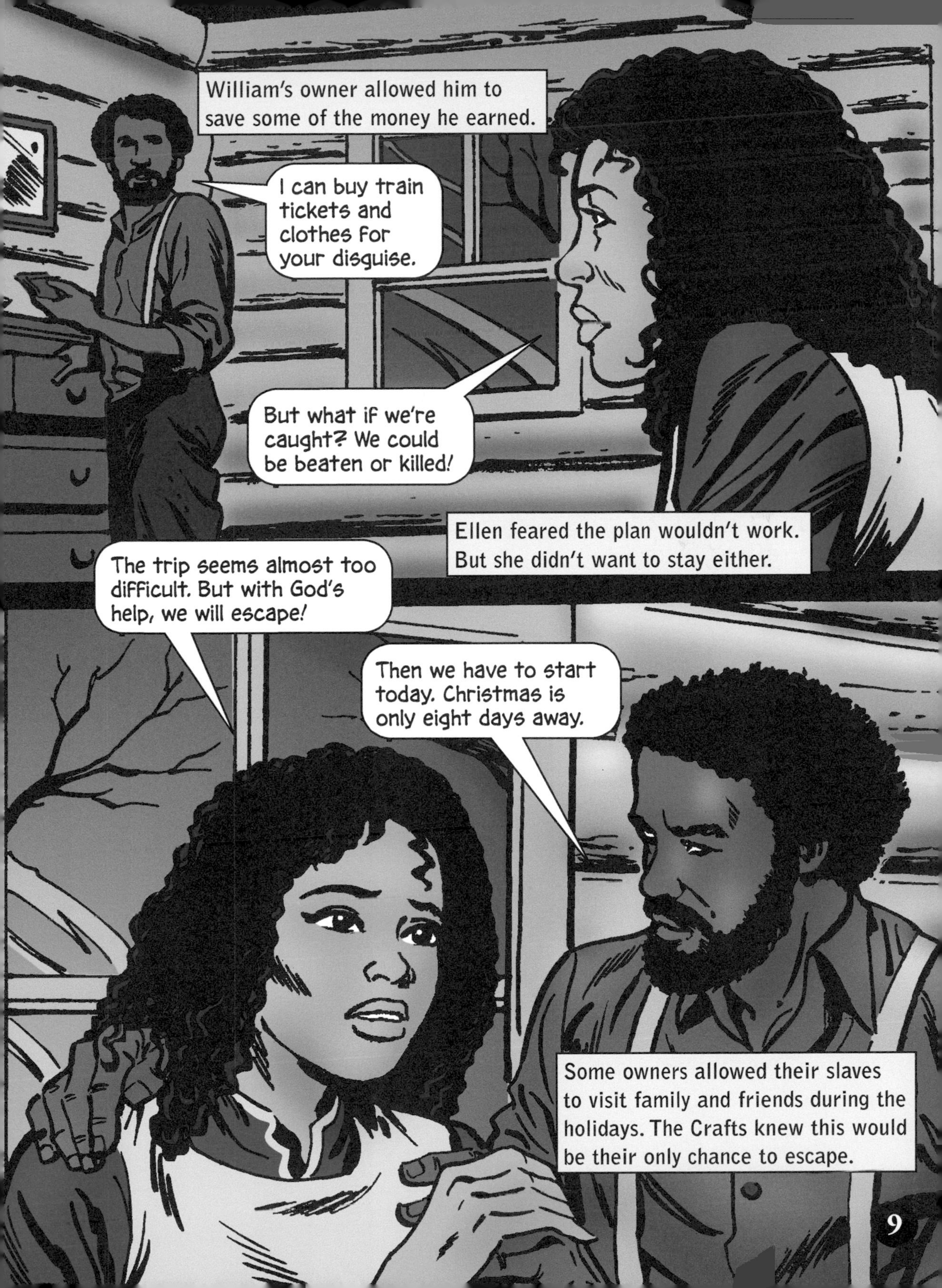
William's owner allowed him to save some of the money he earned.
I can buy train tickets and clothes for your disguise.
But what if we're caught? We could be beaten or killed!
Ellen feared the plan wouldn't work. But she didn't want to stay either.
The trip seems almost too difficult. But with God's help, we will escape!
Then we have to start today. Christmas is only eight days away.
Some owners allowed their slaves to visit family and friends during the holidays. The Crafts knew this would be their only chance to escape.

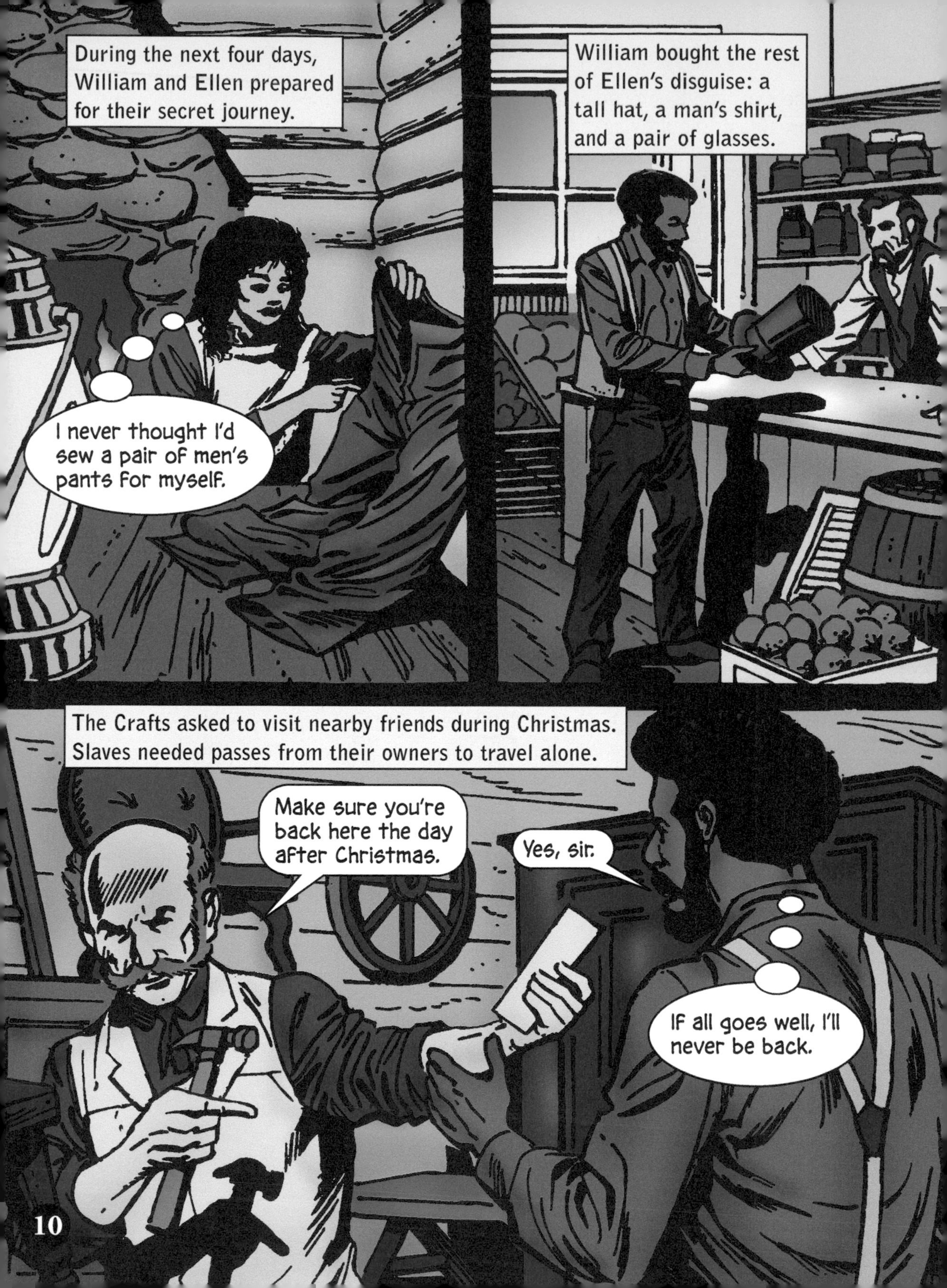
During the next four days, William and Ellen prepared for their secret journey.
I never thought I'd sew a pair of men's pants for myself.
William bought the rest of Ellen's disguise: a tall hat, a man's shirt, and a pair of glasses.
The Crafts asked to visit nearby friends during Christmas. Slaves needed passes from their owners to travel alone.
Make sure you're back here the day after Christmas.
Yes, sir.
If all goes well, I'll never be back.

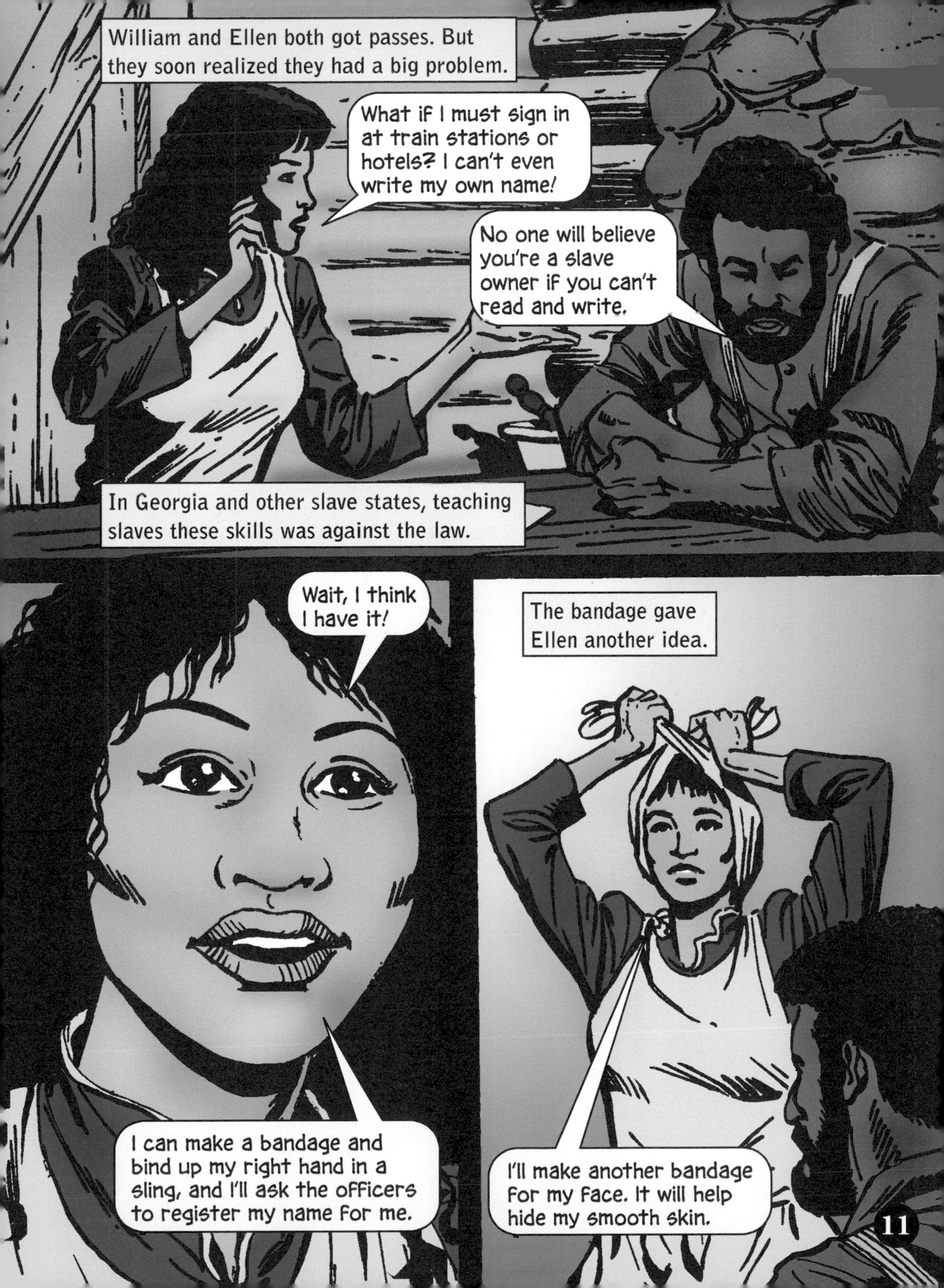
William and Ellen both got passes. But they soon realized they had a big problem.
What if I must sign in at train stations or hotels? I can't even write my own name!
No one will believe you're a slave owner if you can't read and write.
In Georgia and other slave states, teaching slaves these skills was against the law.
Wait, I think I have it!
I can make a bandage and bind up my right hand in a sling, and I'll ask the officers to register my name for me.
The bandage gave Ellen another idea.
I'll make another bandage for my face. It will help hide my smooth skin.

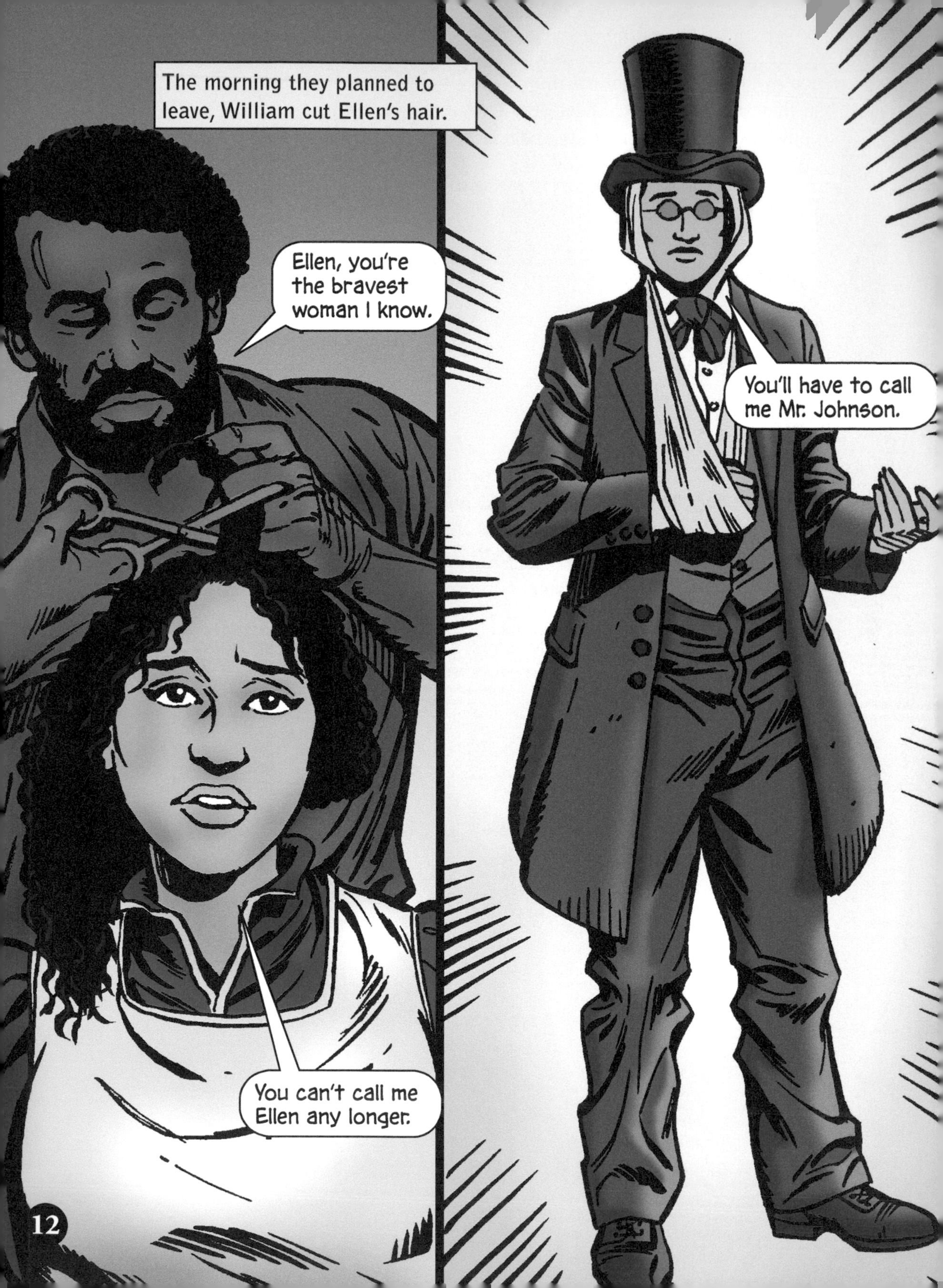
The morning they planned to leave, William cut Ellen's hair.
Ellen, you're the bravest woman I know.
You can't call me Ellen any longer.
You'll have to call me Mr. Johnson.

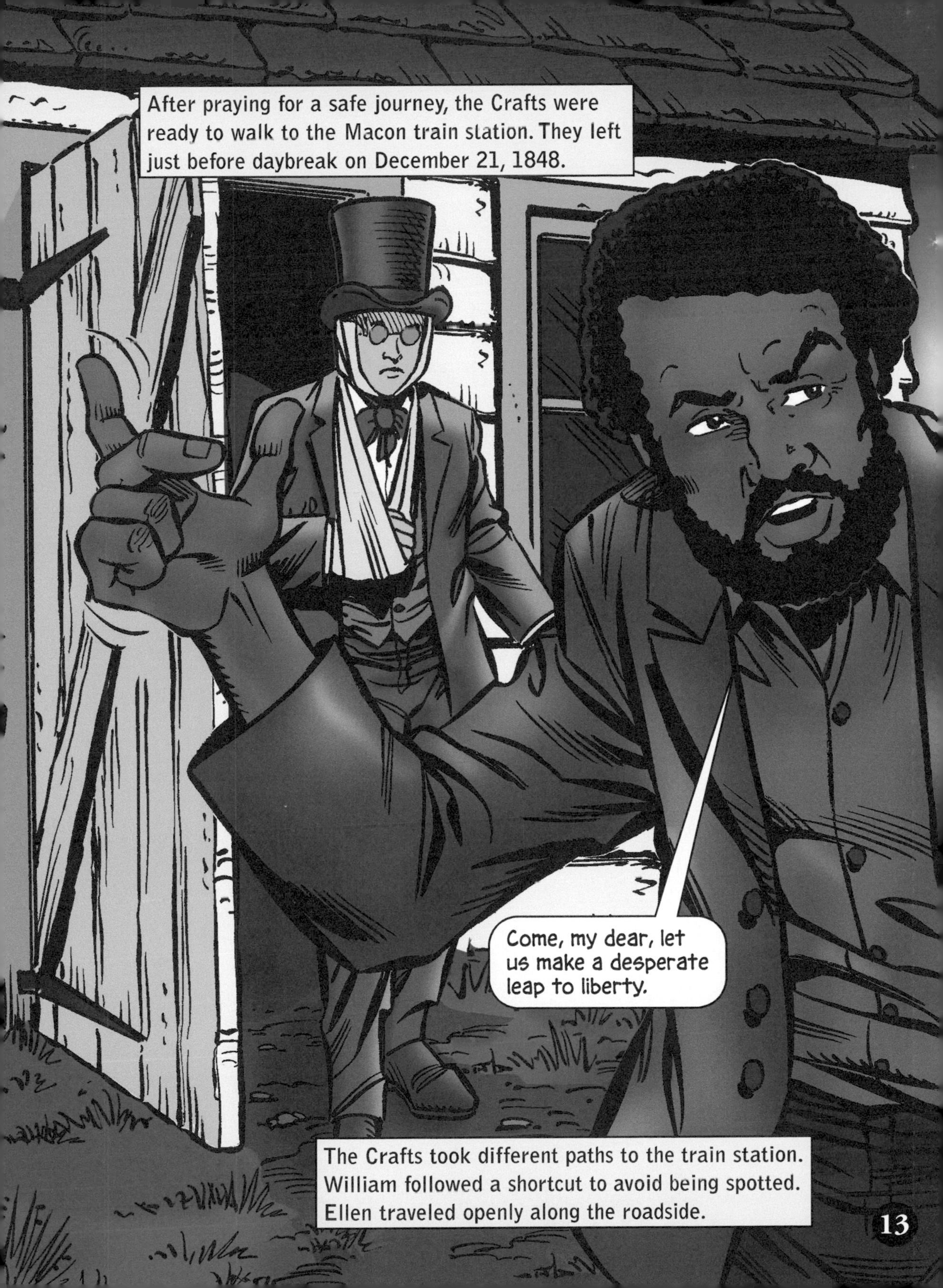
After praying for a safe journey, the Crafts were ready to walk to the Macon train station. They left just before daybreak on December 21, 1848.
Come, my dear, let us make a desperate leap to liberty.
The Crafts took different paths to the train station. William followed a shortcut to avoid being spotted. Ellen traveled openly along the roadside.

CHAPTER 3
TWO TICKETS TO FREEDOM

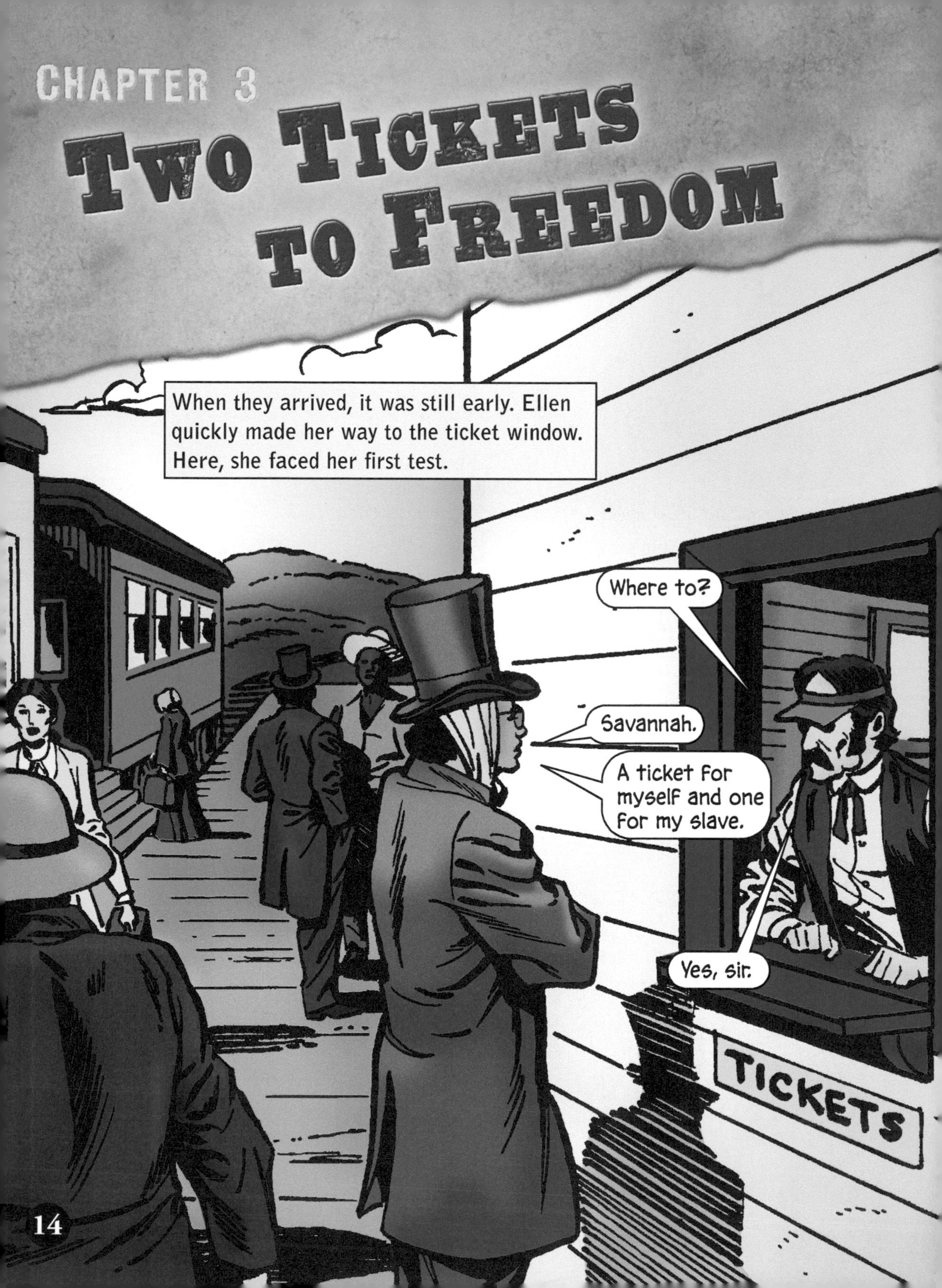
When they arrived, it was still early. Ellen quickly made her way to the ticket window. Here, she faced her first test.
Where to?
Savannah.
A ticket for myself and one for my slave.
Yes, sir.
TICKETS

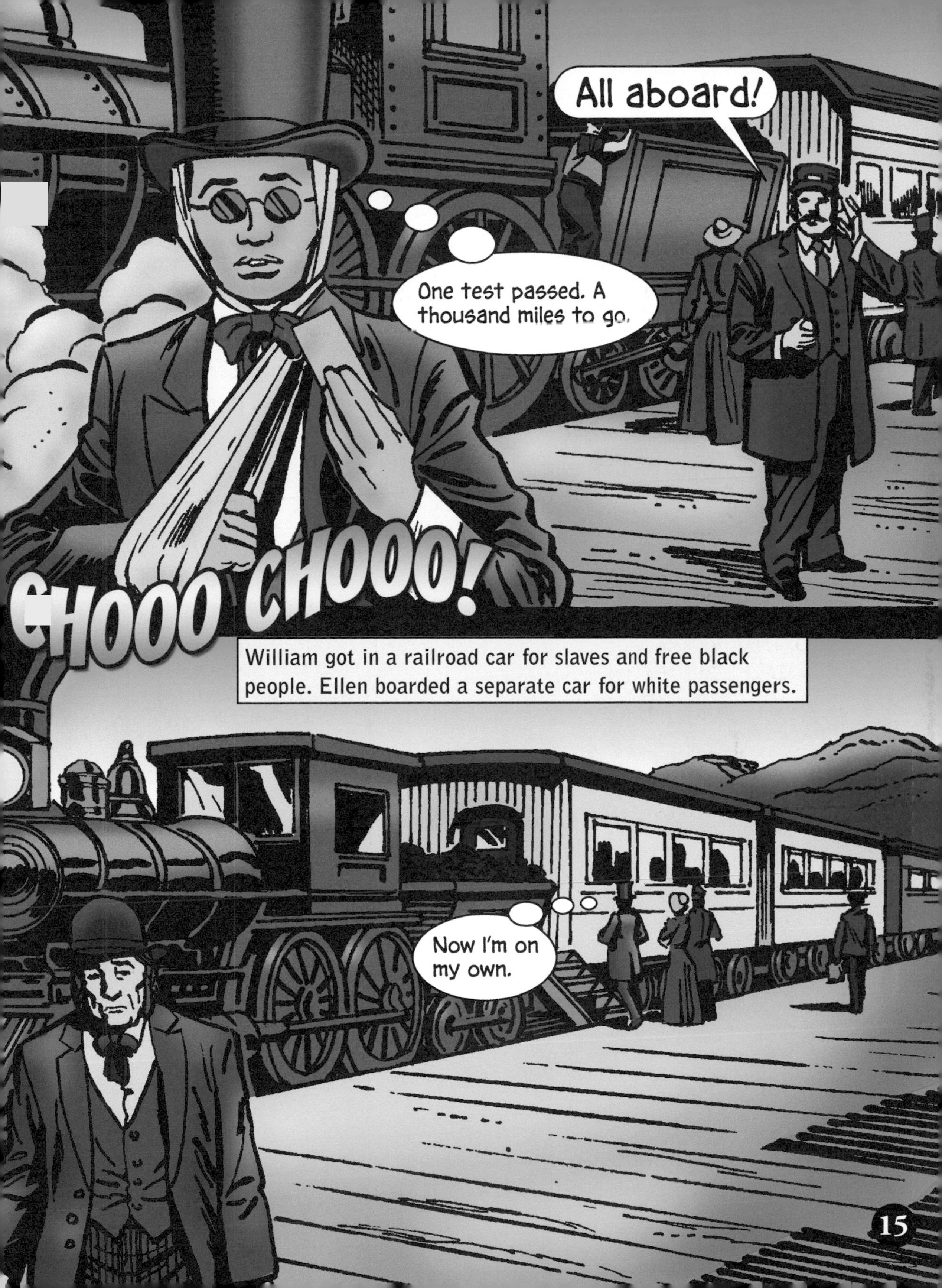
All aboard!
One test passed. A thousand miles to go.
CHOOO CHOOO!
William got in a railroad car for slaves and free black people. Ellen boarded a separate car for white passengers.
Now I'm on my own.

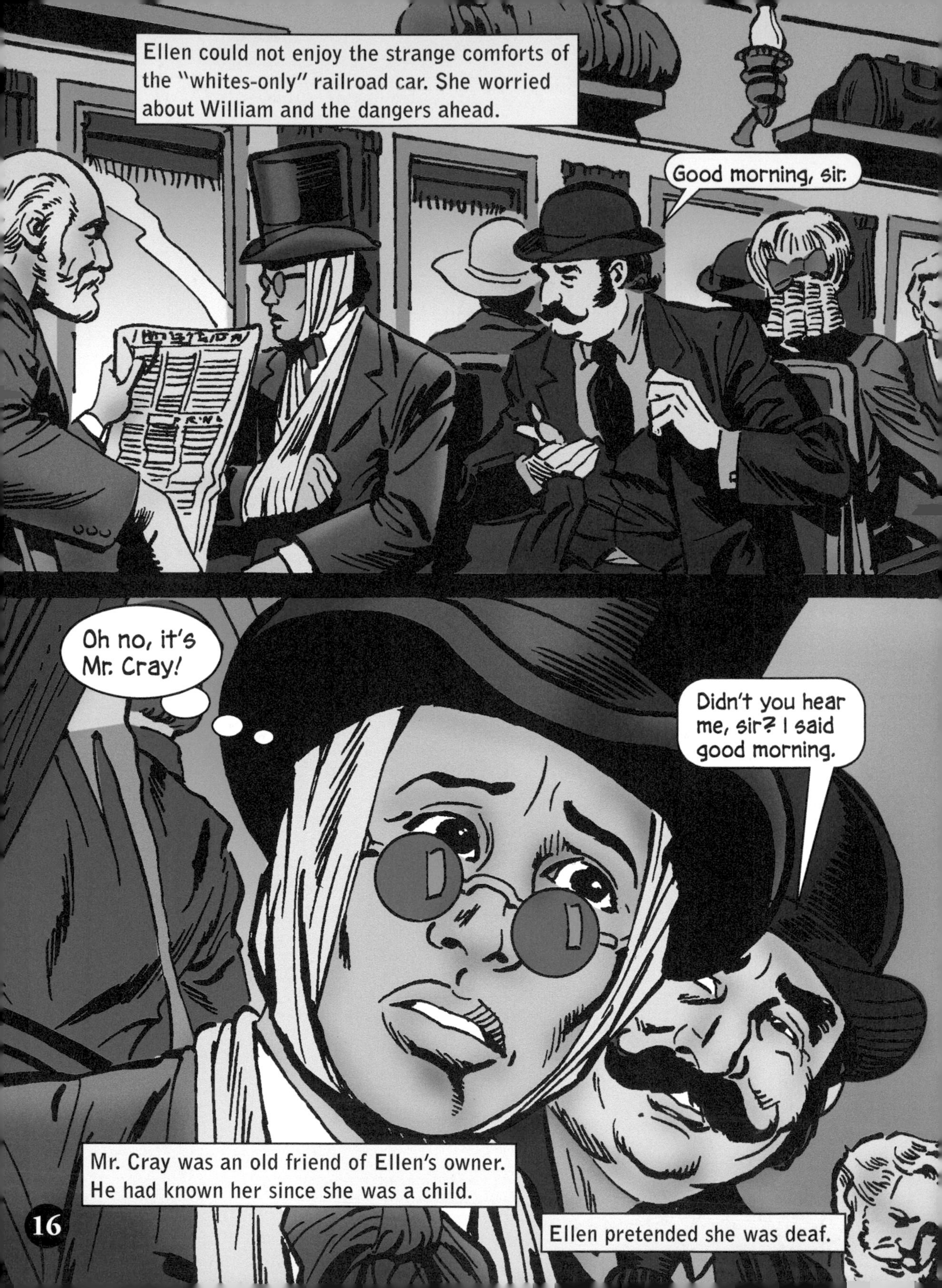
Ellen could not enjoy the strange comforts of the "whites-only" railroad car. She worried about William and the dangers ahead.
Good morning, sir.
Oh no, it's Mr. Cray!
Didn't you hear me, sir? I said good morning.
Mr. Cray was an old friend of Ellen's owner. He had known her since she was a child.
Ellen pretended she was deaf.

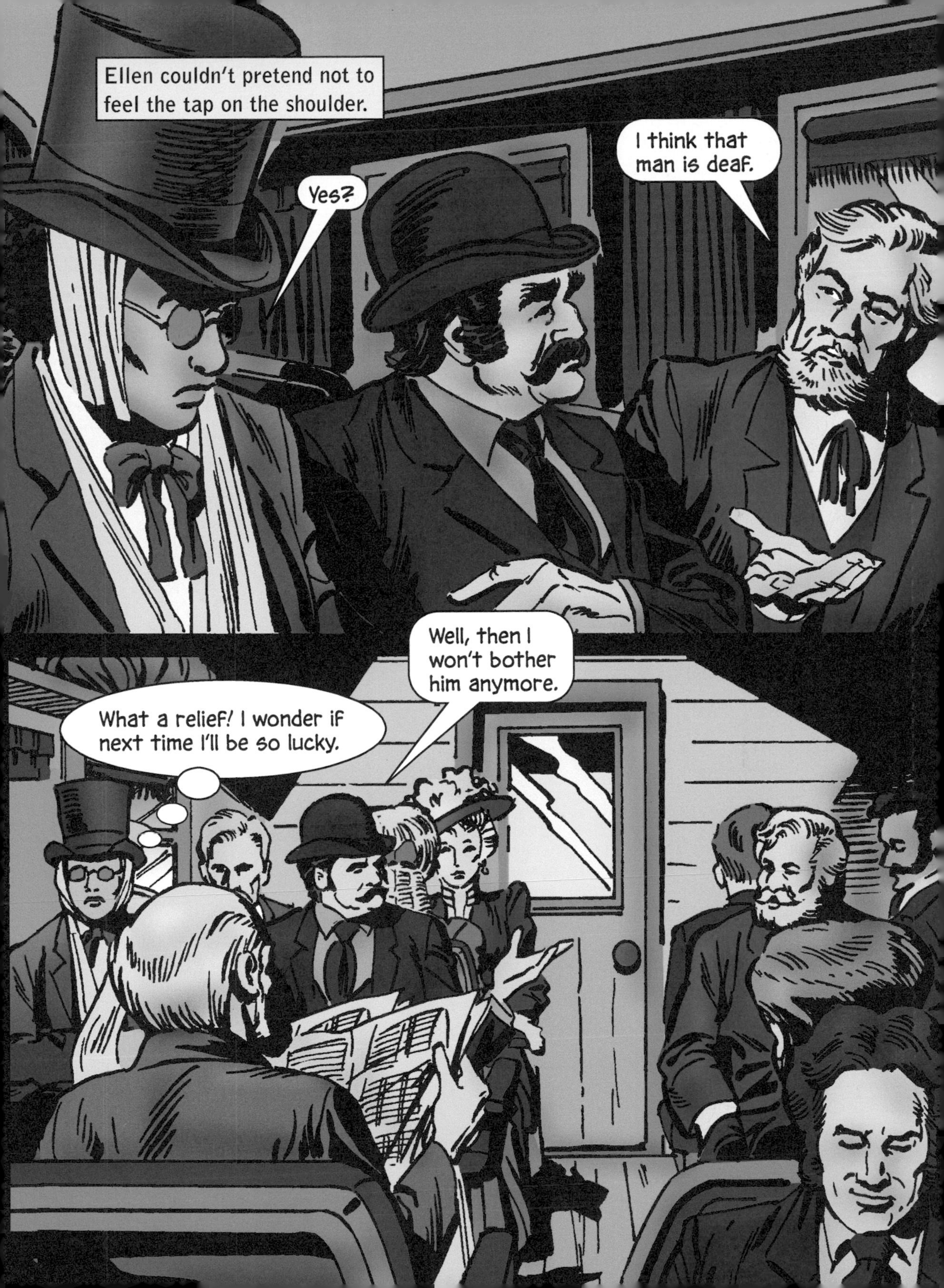
Ellen couldn't pretend not to feel the tap on the shoulder.
Yes?
I think that man is deaf.
Well, then I won't bother him anymore.
What a relief! I wonder if next time I'll be so lucky.

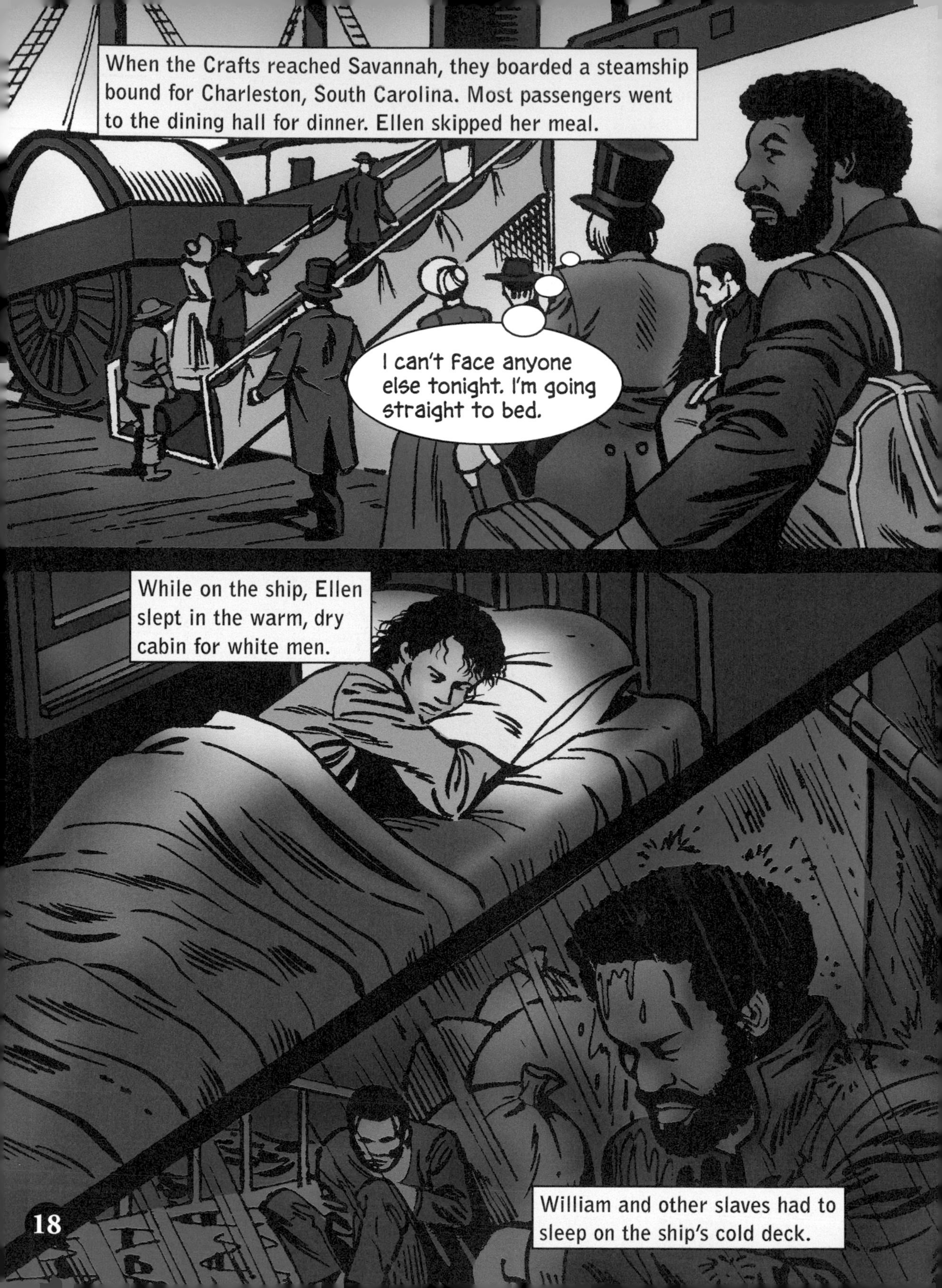
When the Crafts reached Savannah, they boarded a steamship bound for Charleston, South Carolina. Most passengers went to the dining hall for dinner. Ellen skipped her meal.
I can't face anyone else tonight. I'm going straight to bed.
While on the ship, Ellen slept in the warm, dry cabin for white men.
William and other slaves had to sleep on the ship's cold deck.

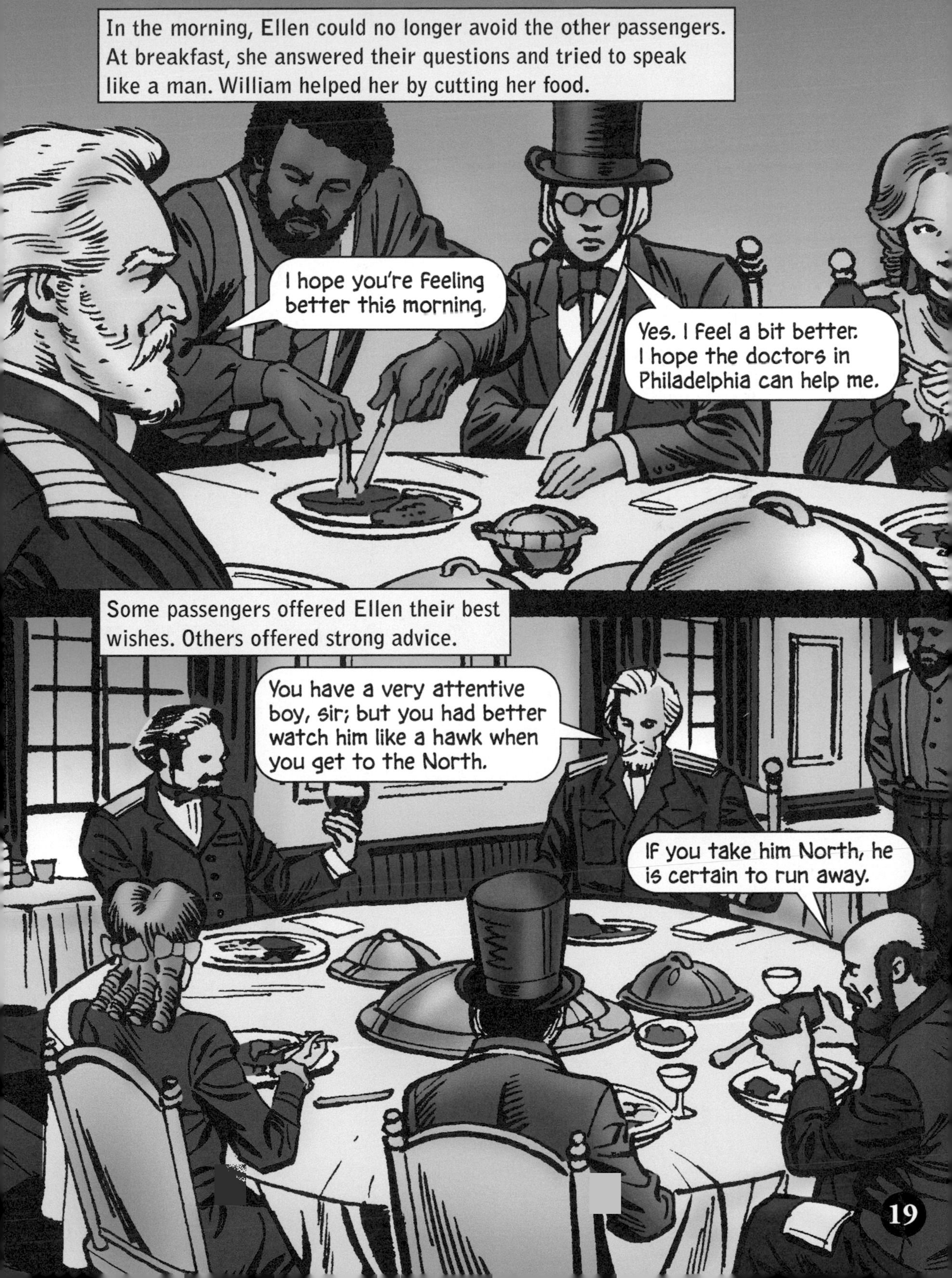
In the morning, Ellen could no longer avoid the other passengers. At breakfast, she answered their questions and tried to speak like a man. William helped her by cutting her food.
I hope you're feeling better this morning.
Yes. I feel a bit better. I hope the doctors in Philadelphia can help me.
Some passengers offered Ellen their best wishes. Others offered strong advice.
You have a very attentive boy, sir; but you had better watch him like a hawk when you get to the North.
If you take him North, he is certain to run away.

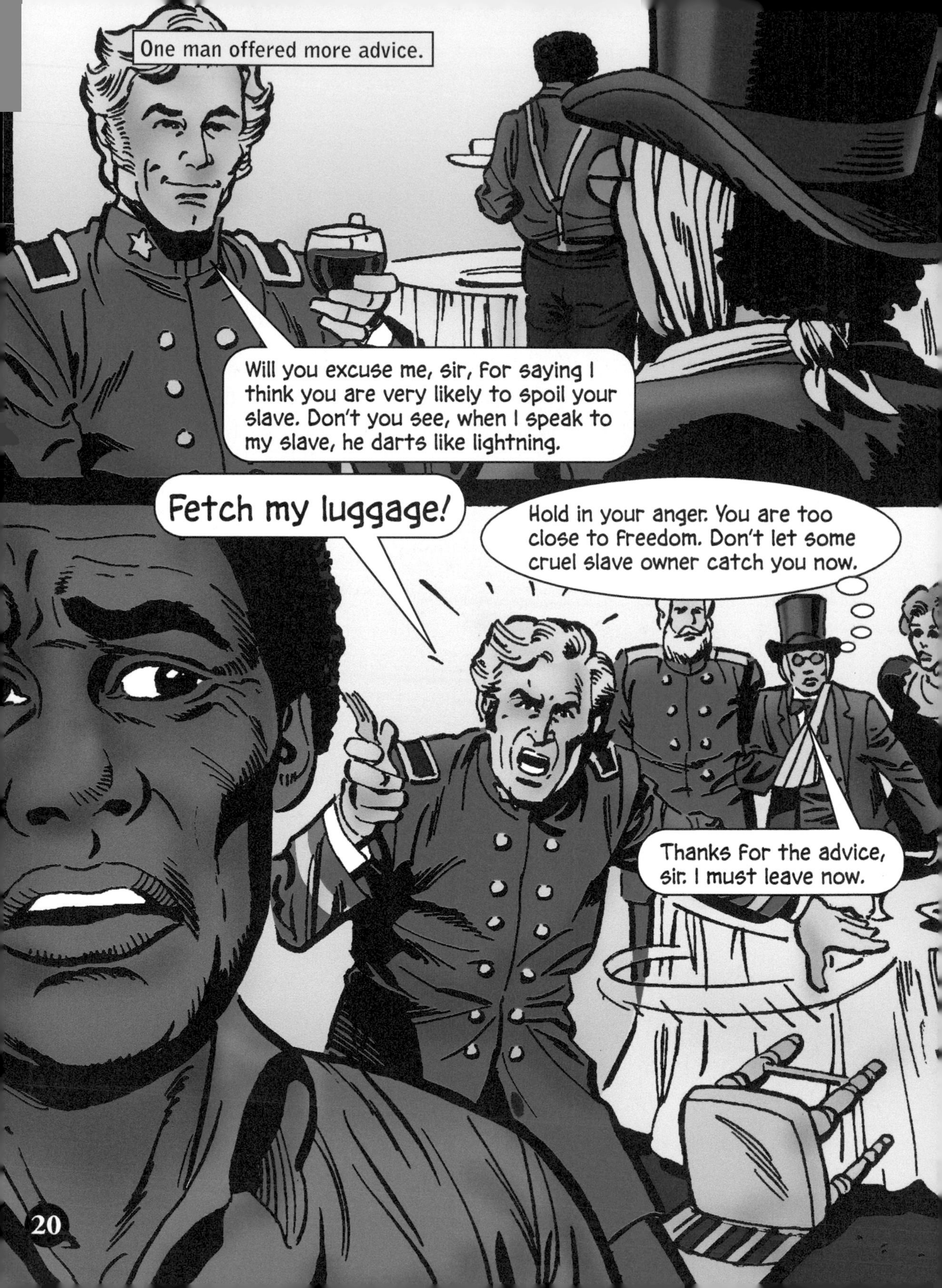
One man offered more advice.
Will you excuse me, sir, for saying I think you are very likely to spoil your slave. Don't you see, when I speak to my slave, he darts like lightning.
Fetch my luggage!
Hold in your anger. You are too close to freedom. Don't let some cruel slave owner catch you now.
Thanks for the advice, sir. I must leave now.

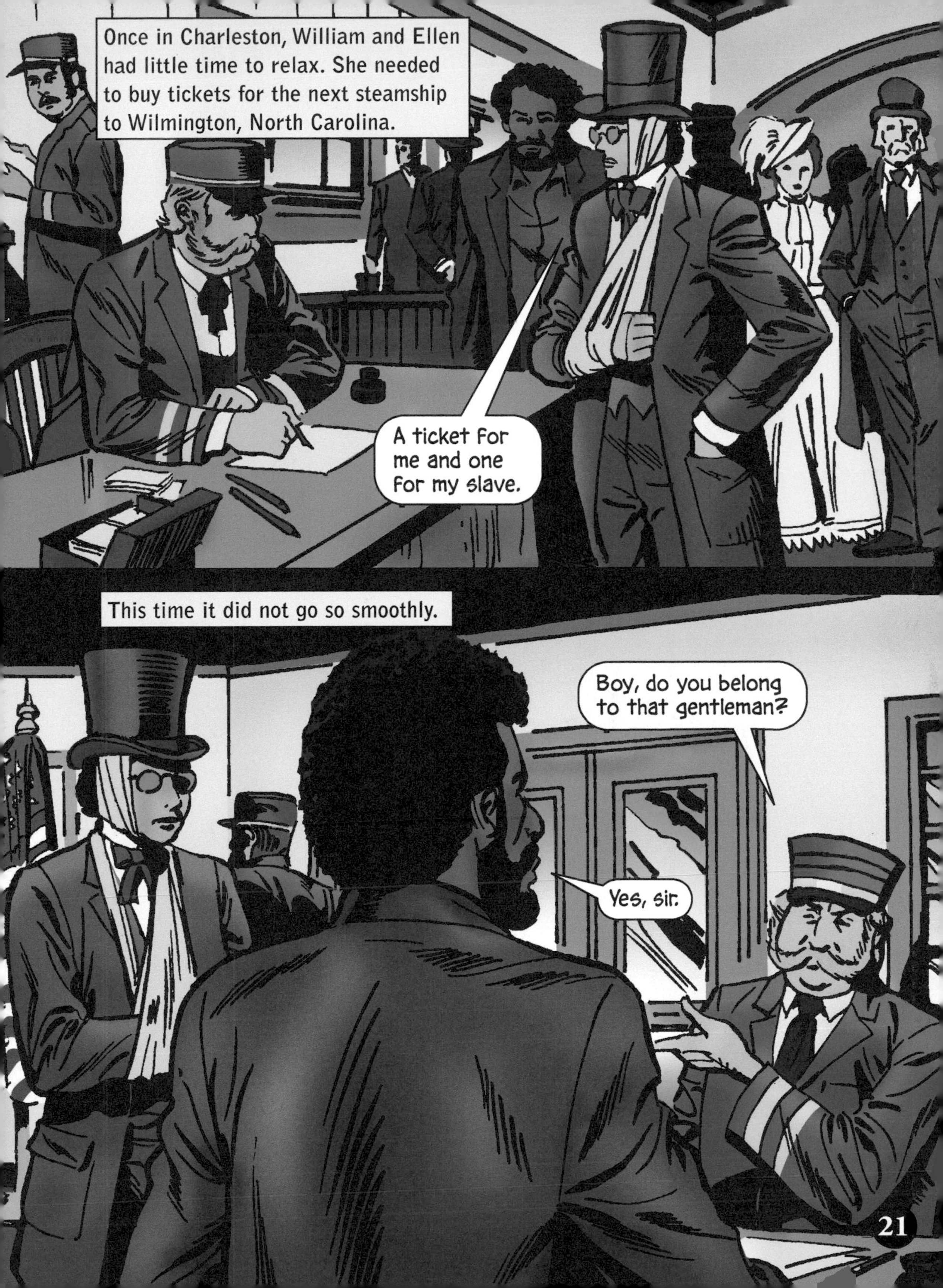
Once in Charleston, William and Ellen had little time to relax. She needed to buy tickets for the next steamship to Wilmington, North Carolina.
A ticket for me and one for my slave.
This time it did not go so smoothly.
Boy, do you belong to that gentleman?
Yes, sir.

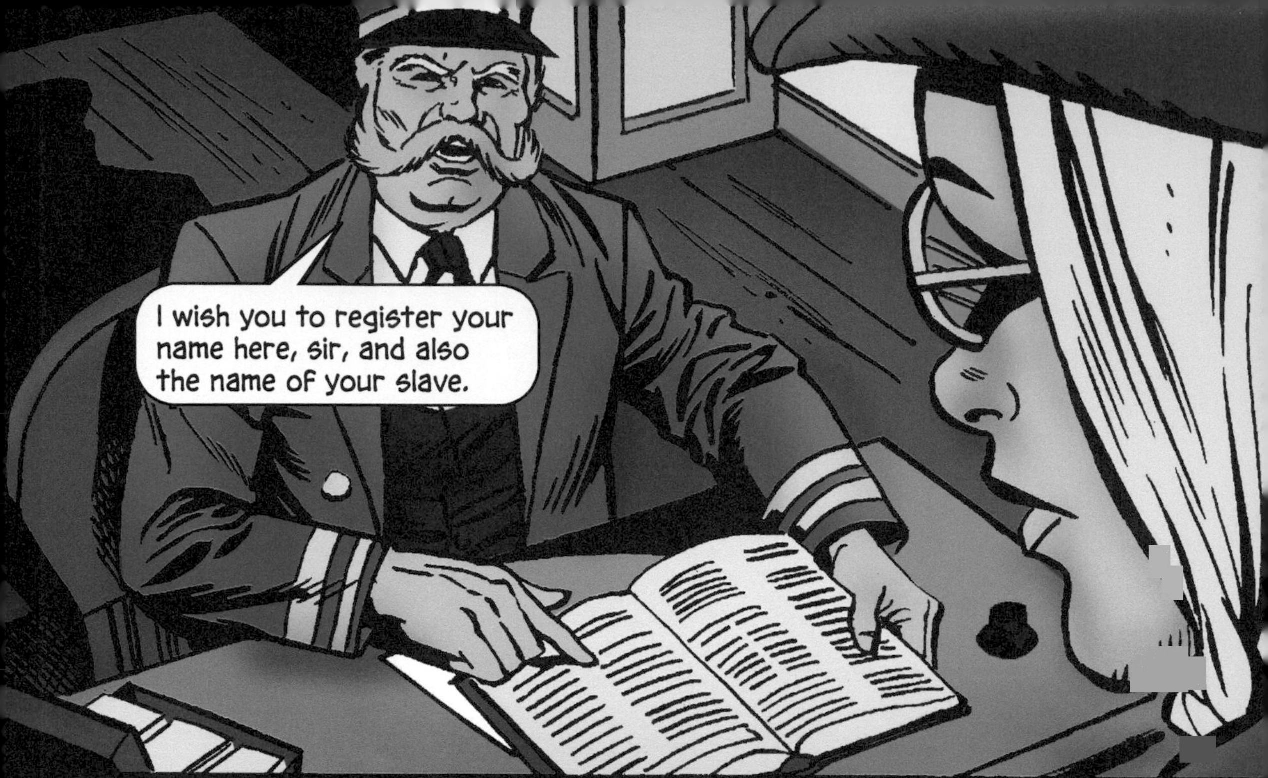
I wish you to register your name here, sir, and also the name of your slave.

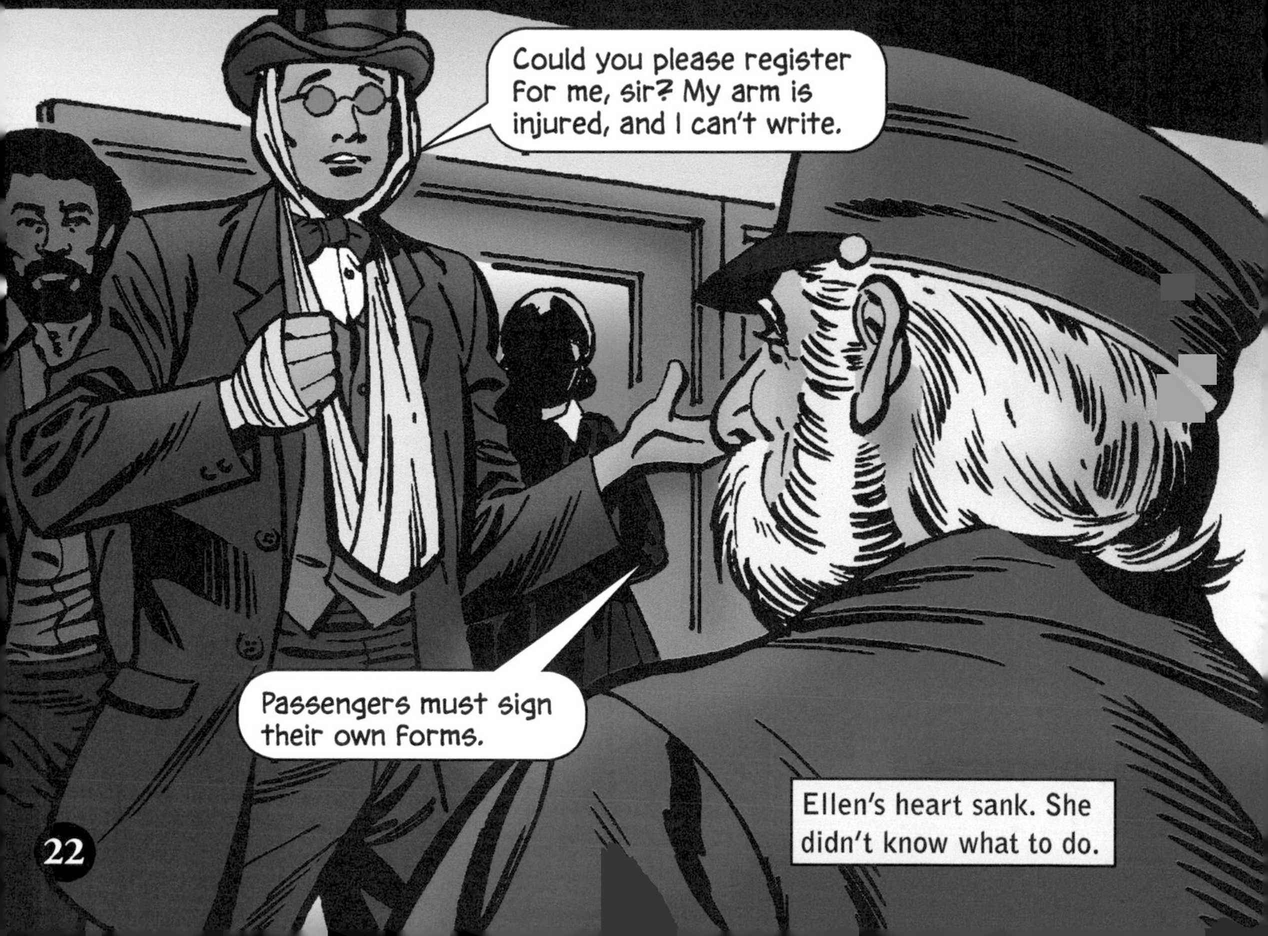
Could you please register for me, sir? My arm is injured, and I can't write.
Passengers must sign their own forms.
Ellen's heart sank. She didn't know what to do.

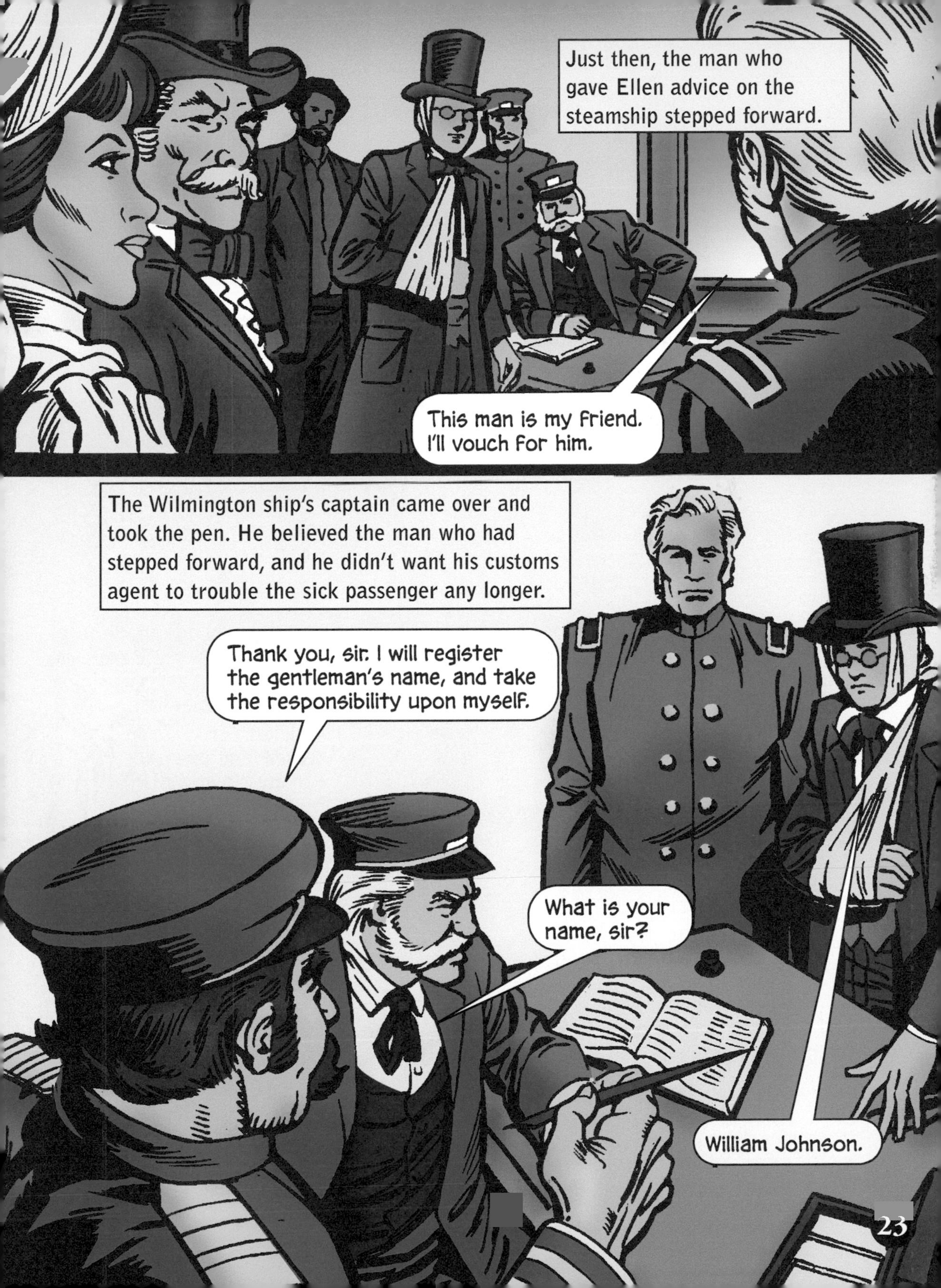
Just then, the man who gave Ellen advice on the steamship stepped forward.
This man is my friend. I'll vouch for him.
The Wilmington ship's captain came over and took the pen. He believed the man who had stepped forward, and he didn't want his customs agent to trouble the sick passenger any longer.
Thank you, sir. I will register the gentleman's name, and take the responsibility upon myself.
What is your name, sir?
William Johnson.

CHAPTER 4

CHRISTMAS IN PHILADELPHIA

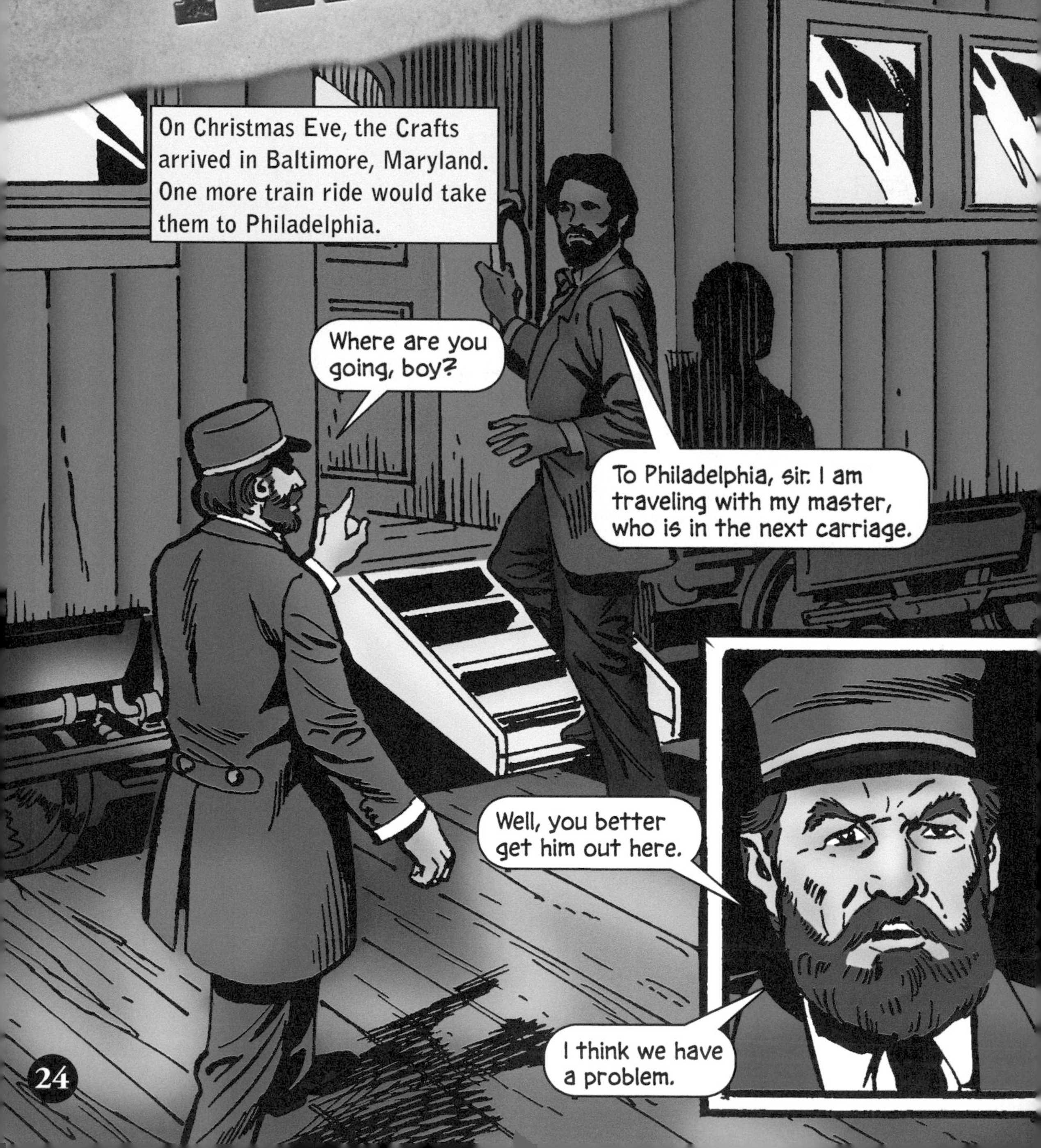
On Christmas Eve, the Crafts arrived in Baltimore, Maryland. One more train ride would take them to Philadelphia.
Where are you going, boy?
To Philadelphia, sir. I am traveling with my master, who is in the next carriage.
Well, you better get him out here.
I think we have a problem.

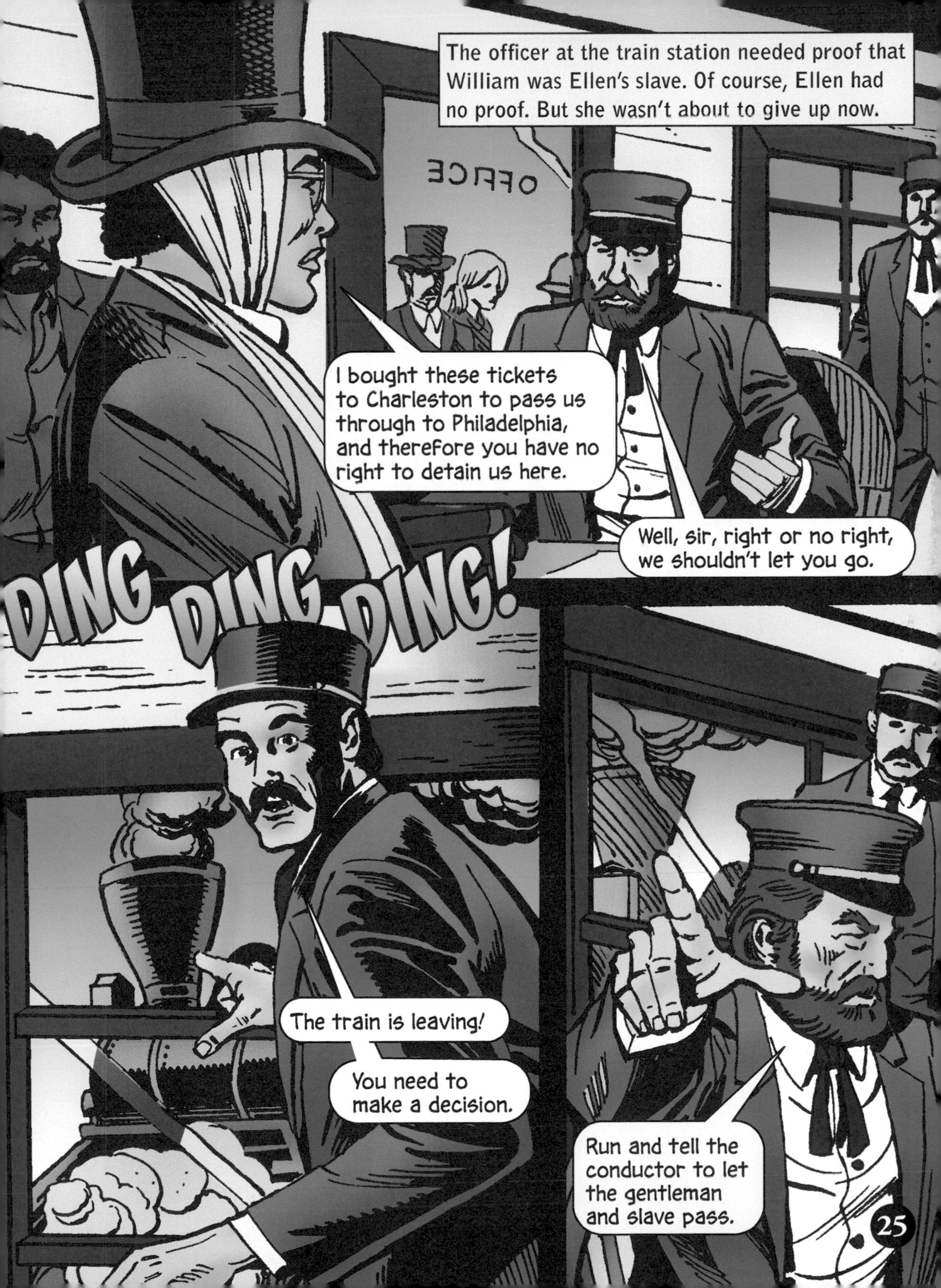

The officer at the train station needed proof that William was Ellen's slave. Of course, Ellen had no proof. But she wasn't about to give up now.
OFFICE
I bought these tickets to Charleston to pass us through to Philadelphia, and therefore you have no right to detain us here.
Well, sir, right or no right, we shouldn't let you go.
DING DING DING!
The train is leaving!
You need to make a decision.
Run and tell the conductor to let the gentleman and slave pass.

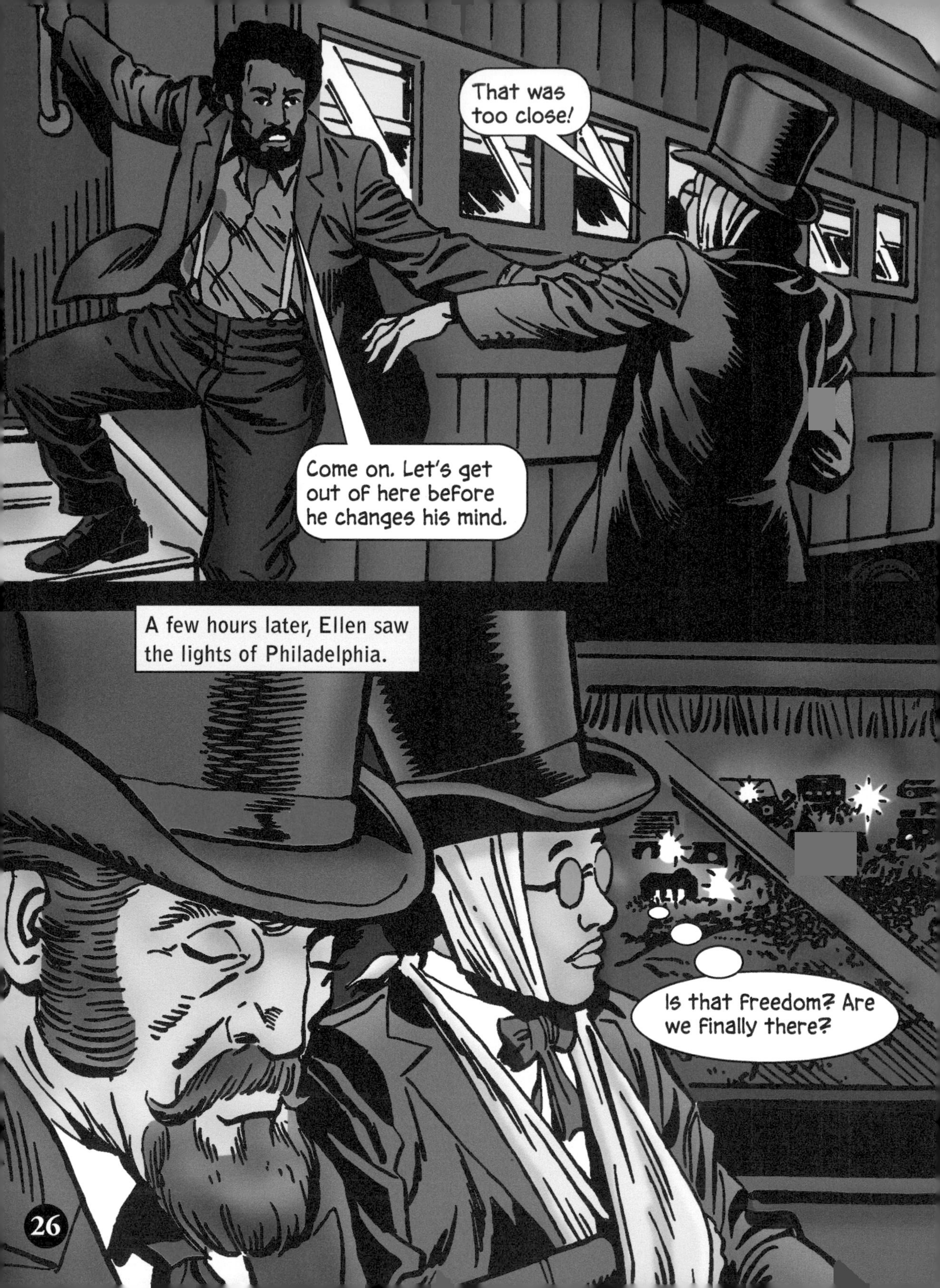
That was too close!
Come on. Let's get out of here before he changes his mind.
A few hours later, Ellen saw the lights of Philadelphia.
Is that freedom? Are we finally there?

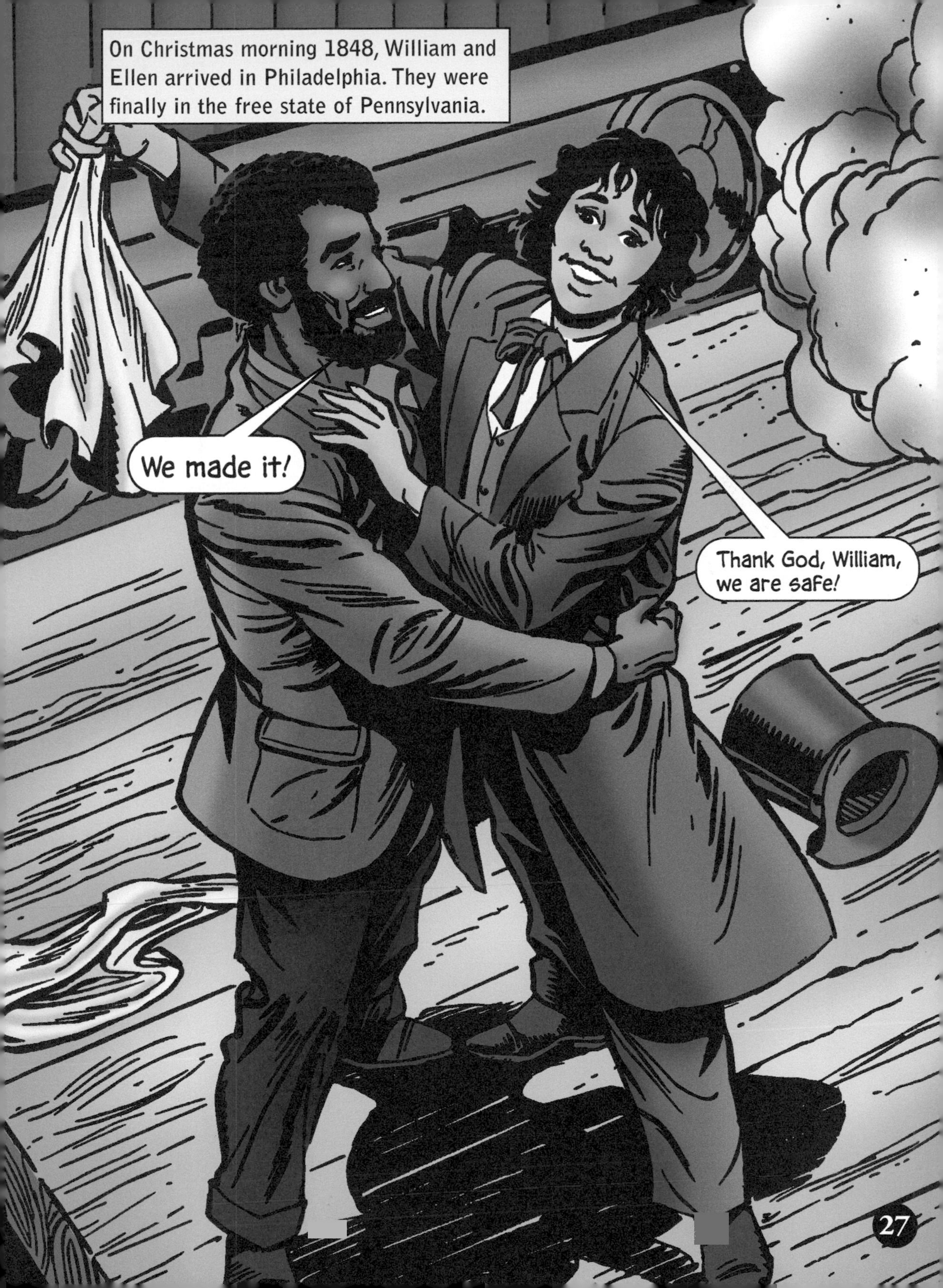
On Christmas morning 1848, William and Ellen arrived in Philadelphia. They were finally in the free state of Pennsylvania.
We made it!
Thank God, William, we are safe!

THE CRAFTS

- Ellen and William Craft eventually had five children. They all grew up free.

- Ellen Craft was born in Clinton, Georgia, in 1826. Her father was James P. Smith, a white slave owner. Ellen's mother, Maria, was one of Smith's slaves. During this time, children of slave women also became slaves.

- William Craft was born into slavery in 1824. At age 16, William watched as his younger sister was sold away at a slave auction. He thought he would never see her again. But they reunited almost 50 years later.

- The Crafts met while living in Macon, Georgia. Around 1846, William and Ellen's owners let them get married and live together. Slave marriages were not legal. They were officially married four years later on November 7, 1850, in Boston, Massachusetts.

- After escaping slavery, the Crafts settled in Boston. William opened a furniture shop, and Ellen made money sewing. The couple joined the abolitionist movement to end slavery and gave speeches about their journey. They hoped their story would help end slavery.

→ In 1850, a revision to the Fugitive Slave Act of 1793 allowed slave owners to hunt for runaway slaves anywhere in the United States. In November 1850, Ellen and William fled to Liverpool, England.

→ As slaves, Ellen and William Craft were not allowed to go to school in the United States. They learned to read and write in England. In 1860, William wrote a book, Running a Thousand Miles for Freedom: The Escape of William and Ellen Craft from Slavery.

→ In 1861, the Northern states began fighting against the Southern states in the Civil War. After the war ended in 1865, Congress passed the 13th Amendment. This addition to the U.S. Constitution ended slavery. Four years later, William and Ellen traveled back to the United States.

→ In 1870, the Crafts returned to Georgia for the first time since their escape. The couple built a home near Savannah. They also started a school for African American children.

→ In 1891, Ellen Craft died at age 65. William died in 1900. He was 76.

GLOSSARY

Congress (KONG-griss)—the government body of the United States that makes laws

Constitution (kon-stuh-TOO-shuhn)—the written system of laws in the United States that states the rights of the people and powers of the government

deaf (DEF)—not being able to hear anything or only hearing very little

disguise (diss-GIZE)—an outfit worn to hide one's identity

register (REJ-uh-stur)—to enter something on an official list

seamstress (SEEM-struhss)—a woman who sews for a living

vouch (VOUCH)—to guarantee that someone is telling the truth

INTERNET SITES

FactHound offers a safe, fun way to find Internet sites related to this book. All of the sites on FactHound have been researched by our staff.

Here's how:

1. *Visit www.facthound.com*
2. Type in this special code **0736849734** for age-appropriate sites. Or enter a search word related to this book for a more general search.
3. Click on the **Fetch It** button.

FactHound will fetch the best sites for you!

READ MORE

Freedman, Florence B. Two Tickets to Freedom: The True Story of Ellen and William Craft, Fugitive Slaves. New York: P. Bedrick Books, 1989.

Isaacs, Sally Senzell. Lite on a Southern Plantation. Picture the Past. Chicago: Heinemann Library, 2001.

Moore, Cathy. The Daring Escape of Ellen Craft. On My Own History. Minneapolis: Carolrhoda Books, 2002.

BIBLIOGRAPHY

Craft, William. Running a Thousand Miles for Freedom: The Escape of William and Ellen Craft from Slavery. Athens, Ga.: University of Georgia Press, 1999.

The New Georgia Encyclopedia. Georgia Humanities Council and the University of Georgia Press. http://www. georgiaencyclopedia.org/nge/Home.jsp

Sterling, Dorothy. Black Foremothers: Three Lives. Old Westbury, N.Y.: Feminist Press, 1988.

Tiffany, Nina Moore. "Stories of the Fugitive Slaves." New England Magazine. January, 1890.

White, Deborah G. Aren't I a Woman?: Female Slaves in the Plantation South. Rev. ed. New York: W.W. Norton, 1999.

INDEX